WILL MY PET BE IN HEAVEN ?

DR. ED KING

Parsons Publishing House

Stafford, Virginia USA

WILL MY PET BE IN HEAVEN?
by Ed King

Parsons Publishing House
P. O. Box 488
Stafford, VA 22554 USA
www.ParsonsPublishingHouse.com
Info@ParsonsPublishingHouse.com

ISBN -13: 978-1-60273-068-7
ISBN -10: 1-60273-068-7
Library of Congress Control Number: 2015936804

Printed in the United States of America.
For World-Wide Distribution.

DEDICATION

This book is dedicated to my son, Marcus, who is waiting in heaven for the time he will be re-united with his family and loved ones, not the least of which is Maggie, the beagle.

TABLE OF CONTENTS

INTRODUCTION

I was very aware of the presence of the Lord in the preparation of this study. Even though this subject may be construed by some as insignificant, I feel it needs to be addressed, if only because I have been asked this question hundreds of times, "Will my pet be in heaven?"

Let me say from the beginning, that we do not, in any way, want to suggest that animals are in the same class or category as human beings. Jesus did not die for animals; it was not necessary because they did not sin. He died for human beings—for us.

I heard some very interesting numbers while preparing for the subject of animals being in heaven. I discovered that there are some 200 billion creatures on this planet for every human. That's right, 200 billion for you and 200 billion for me! I don't know what they all are, and I certainly don't know who did the counting, but the number includes every species, every bug and every bird on the planet. The accuracy of these numbers and the method used to obtain them elude me, but who am I to argue with it? If there are that many, or even a tenth of that number, that is still quite a statement about God's concern for His creation.

There is a great deal that the Bible teaches, both present and future, about the subject of animals so there is no better time to dive into a focused, in-depth study of animals in heaven—a subject on the minds of a great number of people. We love our pets and have become emotionally attached to them and want to believe that they will be in heaven with us, forever. Wouldn't it be great to have some solid truth from the Word of God to back it up? I am confident that you will come away from this book with a new appreciation for Maggie the beagle, Gus the boxer, or your quarter horse out in the stable.

AN UNEXPECTED JOURNEY 1

Have you ever walked into a room and realized that there are great opportunities to enjoy—new and exciting opportunities presenting themselves there? You may anticipate what it's going to be like once you go in and you may even look through a partially open door and see just a little piece—but once you enter you find other rooms and hallways emanating from it. There are beautiful spots opening themselves to you, little surprises, "nooks and crannies" as we say in the south, which would remain unknown unless you carefully examined the area. You could anticipate its contents, but unless you physically entered, you would never really know, precisely, what was there.

That is the way the Word of God is to us. As I was studying the subject of heaven, I discovered some interesting side trips, or new rooms, if you will, presenting me with some new and quite interesting subject matter that I was not fully expecting. I found that here were certain aspects of heaven that were not readily apparent—that were just begging for attention. This book is based on one of those very special side trips that I am confident will be of great interest to you, too. So, let's explore together, in depth, the question, "Will my pet be in heaven?"

I have been researching the subject of heaven for quite some time now. I recently spent two entire days locked away in my study, doing nothing but finalizing my thoughts on a rather sizeable amount of information regarding specific aspects of heaven. The subject is extremely exciting, and there is obviously a great deal to talk about.

I was in the first room, or our main topic area, researching the much broader subject of "Heaven, Our Home," when suddenly, another little room, or subject area began to unfold. "What about animals?" I wondered. "Are there animals there, and if so, what kinds?" This is a subject so remarkably obscure, that I don't know if I would have ever done a study on the subject based on its own merit. It is also amazing just how little teaching there is on the subject—almost a complete void. In my entire life in church, I have never heard this theme addressed. I have heard other people talk about it, and there are some books out there on the subject, but not many. The question of whether or not there are animals in heaven is nearly a neglected subject, and we seem to be somewhat uneasy talking about it.

The King James Version of the Bible is usually the basis of my studies because of its accuracy. In fact, it is one of the most accurate versions that has ever been written. My study tools are geared around it, so I use it as a basis to work from. I use other translations, but I mainly hub around the King James. The problem with the King James Version, in the context of this study, however, is that there are absolutely no references to the word "animal." Not any. You will see the words: "living creatures" and "beast," but unless you understand the context, or understand the Hebrew or Greek behind it, you wouldn't know what was being said.

I recently did some additional reference work from a different translation, which had over five hundred references to the word "animal;" so, the word is definitely in the Bible a great deal. The translation that I used may not be one that you're accustomed to, but the word "animal" is there. Even though animals are mentioned in the Bible a great deal, you could still miss the reference unless you looked for it on purpose. So let's look and see what the Bible says about the subject.

Before we can come to an effective conclusion, however, there is quite a bit that needs to be said as an introduction. We need a solid jumping off point to build a proper foundation, before we take a leap over into what the Scriptures say about animals being in heaven.

WILL MY PET BE IN HEAVEN?

THE ORDER OF CREATION 2

And God said, Let the earth bring forth the living creature after his kind, cattle, and creeping thing, and beast of the earth after his kind: and it was so. And God made the beast of the earth after his kind, and cattle after their kind, and every thing that creepeth upon the earth after his kind: and God saw that it was good. God said let us make man in our image and after our likeness: and let them have dominion over the fish of the sea, and over the fowl of the air, and over all the earth, and over every creeping thing that creepeth upon the earth (Genesis 1:24-26).

The last verse tells us about the creation of man. However, notice that the animals were created just before man.

Animals DO NOT Have a Covenant

Let me say again, in no way do I put animals and humans on the same level. Jesus did not die and shed His blood for animals. He died and shed His blood for men and women—for mankind. Although the Bible talks about the redemption of animals alongside the redemption of man, the relationship is completely different.

Even though there is a very distinct difference, God has placed animals in His earthly creation, just below man—but only just below.

Animals Have Souls

I don't want to get too far ahead of myself here, but I believe the Bible also teaches that animals have a soul.

What do I mean, "have a soul?" I don't believe animals have a soul in the same way that man has a soul; however, the Bible says that God breathed into man and animals the breath of life. This word "breathed" is the Greek word *psuche* (pronounced *soo-kay*) which means "spirit." The implication here is that animals have something divine in them. Rover is not merely a dog that chases squirrels in your backyard; he has God's breath of life in him.

God's Creation—Man's Helpers

Animals were created before man because they were just a little lower in earthly creation, not because they were looked upon as a greater creation. During

6

creation, if you will remember, angels were created just a little lower than man. Man then fell below the angels because he submitted himself to a fallen angel. Man submitted to the devil (satan, formerly known as Lucifer) and sin entered the world. So even though man was created above the angels, he fell below them. Man was created above the animals; but, those animals remained a high form of God's creation.

GOD'S PURPOSE 3

> And the Lord God said, It is not good that
> the man should be alone; I will make him
> an help meet for him. And out of the
> ground the Lord God formed every beast of
> the field (Genesis 2:18-19).

Notice that God said that He would make a helper
"meet" (or able) for man, and following that, we see a
reference to animals. God was saying that He would
make a helper able, or a helper suitable for man.

> And out of the ground the Lord God
> formed every beast of the field, and every
> fowl of the air; and brought them unto
> Adam (Genesis 2:19a).

We now see that the role of the animal kingdom was
to be a helper to man. They were originally brought
into a companionship—a relationship to man—before
sin entered. God's original intention concerning

animals was for them to be a helper suitable to help man in his life's quest—to help him in all of his activities and undertakings.

Animals at Work

I heard a true story about a hospital full of people in critical condition who were all approaching death. At some point, someone in authority made the decision to start bringing domesticated animals, such as dogs and cats, into the hospital to interact with the patients. Can you guess what happened? Statistically provable numbers confirm that the death rate decreased by twenty-five percent just by bringing those animals into the hospital! That should tell you something about the touch of God through animals. In that situation, the presence of the animals improved man's condition.

Think about the helpers that we get from the animal world. Think about a Seeing Eye® dog. A helper suitable. A helper meet. A helper able. That is what "meet" means: able, suitable, or proper.

Think about those incredibly talented drug-sniffing dogs, as well as the bomb-sniffing dogs that help keep all of us safer when we fly, and help take the destructive force of terrorism away from mankind. These great animals, I'm told, have a nose that is 30,000 times more sensitive than a human's nose. The bloodhound breed has a nose that is 80,000 times more sensitive than humans! It is a helper that has been given to man for a valuable purpose.

"Oh, it's just an old dog," you say. Maybe not. I don't think God looks at them like that. God has given us these animals for particular reasons. They were created with a divine purpose and with definite reasons for being here.

There are now dogs that have been trained to detect cancer. The noses of those dogs are so sensitive that they can smell cancerous cells in people, and give caregivers an early warning. Isn't that just like God? You see, animals are helpers for man.

How about lions? "How in the world could a lion help someone?" you ask. Did you know that lions did not eat people before sin entered the earth? You have to remember that a lion, in its present fallen condition, is not the same as God originally created it. The way we see that lion today is quite different from the way we would have seen it, in the original plan God had for it.

The purpose of the entire animal world was to help mankind in all their endeavors. That was the reason that they were created. They were brought to Adam as helpers suitable for his purpose.

ADAM & THE ANIMALS 4

> And out of the ground the Lord God
> formed every beast of the field, and every
> fowl of the air; and brought them unto
> Adam to see what he would call them: and
> whatsoever Adam called every living
> creature, that was the name thereof
> (Genesis 2:19).

Adam did not name any species of the plant world; in fact, you will find that Adam did not name any other form of God's creation, except the animal world. That should suggest to us a special relationship between man and animals. Adam did not name the trees; He named the animals.

God wanted man and animals bonded together in a peculiar, special way. Animals make you laugh. They bring a great deal of joy into your life. They become companions. Animals are extremely loyal, much more so than humans. They depend on us, and in many ways, we depend on them.

You've heard many stories over the past several years, I'm sure, about dogs finding or rescuing people during the aftermath of various terrorist acts. Examples are: the Oklahoma City bombing of the Alfred P. Murrah Federal Building in 1995, the coordinated attacks on the World Trade Center, and the Pentagon on September 11, 2001. These wonderful and talented animals were also ever-present during natural disasters such as Hurricane Katrina in 2005, and others. You have also seen the pictures of dogs sniffing the earthquake rubble in order to help locate the people buried underneath. They are helpers suitable for mankind. They give something very special to us, and we should not ignore it.

Adam was tasked with the responsibility of naming the animals. We see in Genesis chapter two:

> And Adam gave names to all cattle, and to the fowl of the air, and to every beast of the field; but for Adam there was not found a help meet for him (Genesis 2:20).

God told us that the animals were provided in order to help man do various things; but, a better helper was needed for Adam. That is when Eve came into the picture. However, she still did not diminish the role of the animals. Again, animals are not exalted above humans, but we should look upon them properly. Man and the animals were created to have a special relationship.

HOW GOD USES ANIMALS 5

As we look in the book of 1 Kings, we see one example of the many ways that God used animals in the Bible. We have already discovered He used them to make a point to mankind about His nature.

> And it shall be, that thou shalt drink of the brook; and I have commanded the ravens to feed thee there. So he went and did according unto the word of the Lord: for he went and dwelt by the brook Cherith, that is before Jordan. And the ravens brought him bread and flesh in the morning, and bread and flesh in the evening; and he drank of the brook (1 Kings 17:4-6).

This passage is talking about Elijah and what happened when the brook dried up. The ravens were sent by God to feed him; they were helpers suitable for his particular situation.

God used a great fish to help transport Jonah. I don't know if Jonah would have called this help, but it was still a help to God. Jonah wasn't real thrilled about it at the time, but he still got a ride from a fish!

> Now the Lord had prepared a great fish to swallow up Jonah. And Jonah was in the belly of the fish three days and three nights (Jonah 1:17).

As you can see, there is a definite relationship in the redemptive process of man and animals. In the Book of Matthew, we see that God used a fish to pay the taxes of Peter and Jesus.

> Notwithstanding, lest we should offend them, go thou to the sea, and cast an hook, and take up the fish that first cometh up; and when thou hast opened his mouth, thou shalt find a piece of money: that take, and give unto them for me and thee (Matthew 17:27).

God uses animals. He used a fish, in the process of paying taxes. You might say, "He could have done it another way." I guess He could have floated the money to the surface if He had wanted to. He is God after all! Can you imagine how much trouble it would have been for them to go to the bottom of that lake to get the money from that fish? He could have done anything that He wanted to do, but He used the animal kingdom to help man—a helper suitable for man's benefit.

This sounds a little odd, and it is not pleasant in the thought process, but I want to point out to you the beggar Lazarus. God used dogs to help him at his point of need.

> There was a certain rich man, which was clothed in purple and fine linen, and fared sumptuously every day: And there was a certain beggar named Lazarus, which was laid at his gate, full of sores, And desiring to be fed with the crumbs which fell from the rich man's table: moreover the dogs came and licked his sores (Luke 16:19-21).

On the surface, that is downright grotesque. Nevertheless, after some additional research, I found that there are certain healing properties in the saliva of a dog. On a personal level, there is a bigger picture here of the compassion the dogs had for Lazarus. There was no one to comfort him, but the dogs.

When Jesus was baptized by John and was filled with the Holy Spirit, He immediately departed into the wilderness and fasted forty days and forty nights. During that time, because there was no one to comfort Him, Jesus communed and fellowshipped with the animals. Actually, the Bible says "wild animals." Those animals were not wild in the same way we think about a lion, tiger, or a bear; but, more like raccoons and squirrels, and how they are considered to be wild, untamed, and undomesticated animals.

Have you ever watched a squirrel in the yard? You can't tame it easily; I guess you could, but you better start early because they are "wild and woolly!" You can have a lot of fun watching their silly antics. Have you ever fed birds? They are very difficult to tame, but you can get a lot of enjoyment from watching their behavior.

Jesus spent time with the animals during His time of great difficulty, and we see Lazarus comforted by the dogs. You can now recognize that animals bring a lot of comfort into the lives of people at just the right time.

LESSON FROM A LAMB 6

God has created a special relationship between man and the animals. 2 Samuel, the twelfth chapter, bears this out.

> And the Lord sent Nathan unto David. And he came unto him, and said unto him, There were two men in one city; the one rich, and the other poor. The rich man had exceeding many flocks and herds (2 Samuel:12:1-2).

You remember after David had an illicit affair with Bathsheba, Nathan the prophet went to him to straighten out the situation. What Nathan is doing here is drawing an illustration to show David his sin in no uncertain terms. Look at the next verse in the book of 2 Samuel.

> But the poor man had nothing, save one little ewe lamb, which he had bought and

nourished up: and it grew up together with him, and with his children; it did eat of his own meat, and drank of his own cup, and lay in his bosom, and was unto him as a daughter (2 Samuel:12:3).

This man had a sheep that was literally part of his family. I mean a real, "sit at the dinner table with us," part of the family. She was not like one of those sheep outside in the pen; this little sheep was different. Let me be very clear in making the point: there was absolutely nothing improper in this relationship. God used it to illustrate companionship and love between the family and the pet.

God used the bond between a man and an animal to illustrate David's sin—to illustrate what David had done to Uriah. God was endorsing a relationship between a man and a pet. That little sheep ate from his master's table and drank from his cup. Nevertheless, I am confident that there are those of you who would say that you would not want to spoil the animals, and you would never feed them at the table. I'm merely trying to illustrate that this little guy is not just a pen animal; this is a different and special one.

So here is this little lamb that was very close to the poor man and his family—almost like a child would be. The Bible says the lamb was like a daughter to them, being in a very proper relationship. God was illustrating a love relationship that this animal had in the man's home. God really defended it and used it to rebuke David for what he had done to Uriah.

LOVE THY PET 7

My little beagle, Maggie, and I have this funny ritual we go through. I'll ask her, "Would you like a cookie?" The "cookie" is actually our code word for a healthy, but tasty dog treat that she loves. She'll wag her tail and get all excited, and I will give her one. I don't expect you to necessarily understand it, but it doesn't matter; it is just us. She loves it; she thinks it's wonderful.

It is interesting how these animals bond with you and have such a trust in you. They trust you not to hurt them. For instance, I've washed Maggie's face many times in the morning. You heard me, I washed her face! I took a washcloth and washed her face, and she thinks it's great—getting her little beagle face washed. I don't think I would like it if I was a beagle, but she trusts the process. She trusts me to the point that even though something is unpleasant, she is willing to go along with it because I have her best interest at heart.

That is what comes from relationship, and that relationship should never be broken or violated through violence, damage, or pain. There are surely times when your dog needs correction, but you should never hurt him. You don't have to hurt your pet to correct them. Beating is not correcting.

You may think that my little beagle, Maggie, is just an old hound dog, and you would be right, but she is my hound dog. She is a beagle, and she is nosy. That dog actually opens my sock drawer, gets in there, grabs my socks, and brings them to me just to show me what she's done! It's like she's saying, "Hey big guy, look what I did!"

We learned early on that we have to let her go outside to eat; no—actually, we have to let her go outside so we can eat. It is a lot easier on everyone. Because when Maggie is standing on her hind legs, she is just the right size for putting her paws and nose on the dinner table. We will be sitting there enjoying our dinner, and I will casually look over and see her paws and her nose as she peers, just barely, over the top of the table, looking straight at us! Those large, sad, beagle eyes trying to wear me down, hoping for a handout. When she does that, it is one of the funniest things I have ever seen an animal do!

We might be sitting in the den, eating a meal on a tray, and watching something on television. Maggie will come over, stand perfectly still, and put her nose against my leg—she stands completely motionless—

22

just stands there with her nose against my leg. That is my cue to ask her if she wants something.

As you have surely ascertained by now, I'm a big soft-hearted guy when it comes to Maggie, and I'm totally into the relationship with her. You might tell me that you would never give in to your dog that way. However, I would quickly tell you that I "beg" to differ —you would if you had a dog like mine!

Pet Statistics

According to a recent survey of the American Pet Products Manufacturers Association, 60% of the households in the United States own pets. 185 million have freshwater fish, 77.7 million have cats, 65 million have dogs, 17.3 million have birds, 16.8 million have rabbits or gerbils, 8.8 million have reptiles, and 7 million have saltwater fish. Americans love their pets. Mahatma Gandhi said, "The greatness of a nation and its moral progress can be judged by the way its animals are treated." I think there is some truth in that statement. I think he tapped into something.

Now again, remember that I am not trying to put animals in a higher place than they ought to be, but at the same time, we're talking from the Bible. We are not just referencing PETA (People for the Ethical Treatment of Animals). This is not a PETA speech. This is from the Bible. In fact, I cannot even imagine talking about this subject if I had not been studying about heaven.

God told us to care for the animals:

> And God blessed them, and God said unto them, Be fruitful, and multiply, and replenish the earth, and subdue it: and have dominion over the fish of the sea, and over the fowl of the air, and over every living thing that moveth upon the earth (Genesis 1:28).

A Correct Perspective

Therefore, God gave man dominion over the animals, but gave him the responsibility for them, as well. With dominion comes responsibility. When God gives you authority, He expects you to treat it responsibly. We are to steward that responsibility and care for the animals.

Do not misunderstand me. I am not talking about worshipping animals. Domesticated animals are here to serve mankind. Do I believe that it is acceptable to eat meat? Absolutely, because the Bible says that it is. Do I believe it would be right to clothe yourself with an animal skin? I do, in some cases, but not to the destruction of the species. For example, if you were going to kill a cow in order to eat it, why then, wouldn't you want to make shoes out of the hide? I am not trying to be mean or grotesque; I'm just trying to say logically what makes sense. We can sometimes become irrational with this train of thought until we come to the point where we say, "Oh my God, you can't kill any animals!" There are times, however, when it is necessary.

Animals are servants to the human race and are not above us. We do not worship animals.

Statistics tell us that quite often, serial killers, people with a propensity for violence, or sex offenders often get started as smaller children abusing animals. The parallels are shocking.

In the book of Proverbs, Solomon is talking about how we should treat the animals that have been entrusted to us: "A righteous man regardeth the life of his beast: but the tender mercies of the wicked are cruel (Proverbs 12:10).

Many times, the act of mistreating animals follows children into their adult lives. Their violent behavior as a child is sometimes intensified as an adult, and becomes a catalyst in the development of a much more violent nature within them.

The same verse out of the *Good News Bible* says it this way, "Good people take care of their animals, but wicked people are cruel to theirs (Proverbs 12:10, GNB). That tells you a lot. Doesn't it?

The *New Century Version* says it this way, "Good people take care of their animals, but even the kindest acts of the wicked are cruel" (Proverbs 12:10, NCV).

These verses validate the relationship between the mistreatment of animals by young children, and the propensity of them becoming violent adults.

WILL MY PET BE IN HEAVEN?

ANIMALS BELONG TO GOD 8

Animals belong to God. We see this truth in the book of Psalms, chapter fifty.

> For every beast of the forest is mine, and the cattle upon a thousand hills. I know all the fowls of the mountains: and the wild beasts of the field are mine (Psalms 50:10-11).

Since God owns the animals and He gives us stewardship or dominion over them, He expects us to act responsibly regarding them. If something belongs to God, and we abuse it, I would call that sin. Wouldn't you? You might say, "Well, it's just an animal. Who cares?" Evidently, somebody cares. "Just let him stay out in the cold and freeze." I don't think so. There is something about our character and nature that gets expressed at those levels. It says something about us.

To touch an animal in a cruel way is to touch God's possession in a cruel way. It would not be a guiltless act. God has great love for the animals, and so should we.

> "Two sparrows cost only a penny. But not one of them can die without your father knowing it" (Matthew 10:29).

God Loves Animals

> And he said unto them, What man shall there be among you, that shall have one sheep, and if it fall into a pit on the sabbath day, will he not lay hold on it, and lift it out? (Matthew 12:11).

God said that you cannot hide behind your religion. Your religion is not more important than caring for an animal. He said the animal takes precedence over the Sabbath. The observance of the Sabbath does not rule over the caring for the animal.

Before the flood, God did not build the ark for the plants; He built it for the animals. In typology, the flood represents God's judgment upon the earth. God will not judge the earth again with a flood, but He will once again judge it. When man stepped into the ark he floated above the judgment. The rapture of the church is God taking man out above His judgment. So the ark represents the rapture of the church or the removal of man from judgment. Noah had a lot of company in the ark—not just his family, but a great many animals. So, is it possible that there could be resurrected animals at the resurrection?

And the Lord said unto Noah, Come thou and all thy house into the ark; for thee have I seen righteous before me in this generation. Of every clean beast thou shalt take to thee by sevens, the male and his female: and of beasts that are not clean by two, the male and his female. Of fowls also of the air by sevens, the male and the female; to keep seed alive upon the face of all the earth. Some animals were brought in in sevens and some animals were brought in in twos (Genesis 7:1-3).

Animals and the Sabbath

God spared the animals during His time of judgment upon the earth. We also find that animals were included in the observation of the Sabbath.

Remember the sabbath day, to keep it holy. Six days shalt thou labour, and do all thy work: But the seventh day is the sabbath of the Lord thy God: in it thou shalt not do any work, thou, nor thy son, nor thy daughter, thy manservant, nor thy maidservant, nor thy cattle, nor thy stranger that is within thy gates: For in six days the Lord made heaven and earth, the sea, and all that in them is, and rested the seventh day: wherefore the Lord blessed the sabbath day, and hallowed it (Exodus 20:8-11).

Here are the same verses from the *Good News Bible*:

> Observe the Sabbath and keep it holy. You have six days in which to do your work, but the seventh day is a day of rest dedicated to me. On that day no one is to work—neither you, your children, your slaves, your animals, nor the foreigners who live in your country. In six days I, the Lord, made the earth, the sky, the seas, and everything in them, but on the seventh day I rested. That is why I, the Lord, blessed the Sabbath and made it holy (Exodus 20:8-11, GNB).

God says that the animals were definitely included in the religious observation of the Sabbath. God looked at the animals as a part of His religious celebration and process.

AWAY IN A MANGER 9

Who was present at the birth of Jesus? As you remember, the world did not want anything to do with Him. There was no room for Mary and Joseph in the inn so they went to the animal's stable. Very much, like Lazarus and the dogs, the animals comforted them. This was no small thing. Animals were included in the holy observance of the Sabbath. You could also say that animals were included in praising God.

Do Animals Really Praise God?

> Praise the Lord from the earth, ye dragons, and all deeps: Fire, and hail; snow, and vapours; stormy wind fulfilling his word: Mountains, and all hills; fruitful trees, and all cedars: Beasts, and all cattle; creeping things, and flying fowl (Psalm 148:7-10).

The Living Bible translates it this way:

And praise him down here on earth, you
creatures of the ocean depths. Let fire and
hail, snow, rain, wind, and weather all obey.
Let the mountains and hills, the fruit trees
and cedars, the wild animals and cattle, the
snakes and birds (Psalm 148:7-10).

Notice, it says to praise the Lord down here on the
earth. Here. Now. The reference is to animals. The
Bible says animals, according to God, are part of the
praise process. Part of the worship of God is done
through the animals. Not all of it, but a portion of it.

You might say, "Animals are nothing." Well, God
certainly doesn't look at them as "nothing." If you
really think about this and the sacrifices that were
made prior to the time of Jesus, it was the blood of a
bull, a goat, a heifer, a lamb, a turtledove, and others
that cleansed man from sin. Sometimes we think
animals shed their blood and gave their life because
they were dispensable—they didn't matter, but
remember that God said to never bring a sacrifice or
offering to Him that was unworthy. We studied earlier
that the animals were created just below man. The only
reason that an animal could be a substitute for Jesus
before He came was because animals had such a value
to God. He saw them as an acceptable offering, used in
a religious observance.

That revelation should change the way we think about
animals a little, shouldn't it?

So animals, in a sense, and to a degree, are holy. Again,
do not misunderstand anything that I'm saying here.

Animals are not holy like men are holy, but animals to a degree are holy to God. They are a high form of His creation, and they are offering praise to God.

The Bible says, "Let every thing that hath breath praise the Lord. Praise ye the Lord" (Psalm 150:6). You think animals breathe? God breathed into them the breath of life. The same God that breathed the breath of life into them declared that everything that has breath should praise the Lord.

Genesis chapter three talks about some animals that could actually speak:

> Now the serpent was more subtil than any beast of the field which the Lord God had made. And he said unto the woman, Yea, hath God said, Ye shall not eat of every tree of the garden? And the woman said unto the serpent, We may eat of the fruit of the trees of the garden: But of the fruit of the tree which is in the midst of the garden, God hath said, Ye shall not eat of it, neither shall ye touch it, lest ye die. And the serpent said unto the woman, Ye shall not surely die (Genesis 3:1-4).

Here we have a conversation going on between Eve and the serpent, which we know to be the devil. There is the assumption, many times, that when you see the word "serpent," you visualize a snake or reptile of some sort. It might not have been a snake, but that's the way we normally picture it. Here we have the interaction between Eve and the serpent with the assumption that this snake was suddenly possessed by the devil and began to talk. That is not what this Scripture seems to indicate, however. Eve was not the least bit upset or caught off guard, wondering why the serpent could talk. The serpent evidently had spoken to her on other occasions in the past.

TALK TO THE ANIMALS 10

We get these glimpses of God's creation talking today in the form of a parrot or a mynah bird since they have the ability to speak. Moreover, chimpanzees and other apes have been trained to use sign language to communicate with their trainers—some with a vocabulary of over one hundred and thirty words.

Animals are not as intelligent as humans in some ways. In other ways, however, they are actually more intelligent. For example, they have stronger instincts, and their sense of smell is up to 80,000 times greater than a human's sense of smell. Conversely, an animal's ability to reason is not as strong as a human's reasoning ability. They do not have the capacity to evaluate and use information as well as we do, but their instincts are exceptional. Experts say that during the tsunami in Indonesia, none of the animals were killed because they had already gone to higher ground. Conversely, none of the people made that trip to higher ground a priority. The animals instinctively knew that something very much out of the ordinary was getting ready to happen, and they acted accordingly. The Bible tells us to learn from the animals for very good reasons.

Sometimes, we may scold our animals for reacting to something that we are not aware of, or doing certain things that we don't understand. For instance, we might buy a dog to watch our homes, but when it starts barking, we scold him! Maybe there is some warning there from the Lord.

A Talking Donkey

We see another glimpse of this with Balaam's donkey. Balaam was about to do some things that were angering the Lord, so the Lord had to get a message to him.

> And God's anger was kindled because he went: and the angel of the Lord stood in the way for an adversary against him. Now he was riding upon his ass, and his two servants were with him. And the ass saw the angel of the Lord standing in the way, and his sword drawn in his hand: and the ass turned aside out of the way, and went into the field: and Balaam smote the ass, to turn her into the way (Numbers 22:22-23).

So this donkey began to see things that Balaam could not see. Balaam was trying to get the donkey to do certain things, but the donkey did not want to respond.

> But the angel of the Lord stood in a path
> of the vineyards, a wall being on this side,
> and a wall on that side. And the Lord
> opened the mouth of the ass, and she said
> unto Balaam, What have I done unto thee,
> that thou hast smitten me these three
> times? (Numbers 22:24, 28).

I want you to notice something. The donkey did not
say to Balaam, "Can't you see the angel?" The donkey
responded to him with concern for their relationship,
"Why do you keep hitting me?" Now, look at what
happened next.

> And the ass said unto Balaam, Am not I
> thine ass, upon which thou hast ridden ever
> since I was thine unto this day? Haven't I
> served you? What are you hitting me for?
> (Numbers 22:30).

Was this a prophetic word coming from the donkey?
No, it was not. It was a relationship word coming from
the donkey. You see, animals know much more than we
give them credit for. They might not be able to
verbalize things, but the awareness is there.

> Then the Lord opened the eyes of Balaam,
> and he saw the angel of the Lord standing
> in the way, and his sword drawn in his
> hand: and he bowed down his head, and fell
> flat on his face. And the angel of the Lord
> said unto him, Wherefore hast thou smitten
> thine ass these three times? behold, I went

out to withstand thee, because thy way is
perverse before me: And the ass saw me,
and turned from me these three times:
unless she had turned from me, surely now
also I had slain thee, and saved her alive
(Numbers 22:31-33).

In other words, the angel would have killed Balaam
and saved the donkey! That donkey saved Balaam's life.
They are a helper suitable for what you need at any
moment in time.

"And Balaam said unto the angel of the Lord, I
have sinned" (Numbers 22:34).

Usually, when we read that story, we always talk about
Balaam disobeying God and the talking donkey. And
we joke about it and laugh; we may utter the witty
comment, "Maybe there's hope for us!" We know that
the donkey is not as intelligent as a human —and God
historically does use people more than He uses
donkeys—but, we do see that the relationship was
based on the donkey and Balaam. The conversation
was not, "Thus saith the Lord, there is an angel in the
path. Back up, back up, back up. You may be killed at
any moment!" No, it was the donkey asking Balaam
why he was hitting her. It was the angel that gave him
the word about what God was doing. The donkey was
talking to Balaam about how they were relating.

THE NATURE OF GOD 11

> For the invisible things of him from the creation of the world are clearly seen, being understood by the things that are made, even his eternal power and Godhead; so that they are without excuse (Romans 1:20).

This verse is talking about God's witness to the world. There is a hard-headed world that will not read the Bible and does not believe in God; but, there is a testimony of God's goodness, a testimony of God's nature, a testimony of God's character that is out there in the world, too, whether they want to believe it or not.

The first chapter of Romans in the New International Version says it this way:

> For since the creation of the world God's invisible qualities—his eternal power and

divine nature—have been clearly seen, being understood from what has been made, so that people are without excuse (Romans 1:20).

God's creation, in all of its forms, reveals the nature of God to us—it reveals what God is like. A beautiful flower, a beautiful sunset, or the character of different animals are all expressions of the nature of God. The animal kingdom was intended to be an expression of Him before sin entered, but man's sin has certainly affected them. With that in mind, let's look at the book of Job.

The Book of Job

Here we find that God is speaking directly to Job: "Hast thou given the horse strength? hast thou clothed his neck with thunder?" (Job 39:19).

God is asking Job if he was the one that gave strength to the horse. The answer is clearly no. The obvious answer being, "Who else but God could do that?" This is the nature of God in a horse. God's nature is seen in His creation, the aspects of God's nature. The expression of His nature in a flower is not the same as the expression of His nature in a horse, but there are similar facets or aspects in each. That dog that gives you joy is an expression of God's joy. The bird's silly antics that make you laugh, is an expression of God's sense of humor.

Let's stay with Job in the thirty-ninth chapter:

Hast thou given the horse strength? hast thou clothed his neck with thunder? Canst thou make him afraid as a grasshopper? the glory of his nostrils is terrible. He paweth in the valley, and rejoiceth in his strength: he goeth on to meet the armed men. He mocketh at fear, and is not affrighted; neither turneth he back from the sword. The quiver rattleth against him, the glittering spear and the shield. He swalloweth the ground with fierceness and rage: neither believeth he that it is the sound of the trumpet. He saith among the trumpets, Ha, ha; and he smelleth the battle afar off, the thunder of the captains, and the shouting (Job 39:19-25).

These passages concerning the horse speak of the nature of God. The bravery of the horse expresses to people the connection with God's character: "You don't scare me. I'm not afraid of you. I will go to battle with you." That is an expression of the nature of God.

Look at the next verse, "Doth the hawk fly by thy wisdom, and stretch her wings toward the south?" (Job 39:26).

In other words, did you teach the birds how to fly south, or did God? Do I believe that maybe little Maggie the beagle, who stands at the table with her paws and her nose barely resting on top, is an expression of God? I believe she is. And it is obviously not because God is a beagle, nor because He is begging for food. It is because God wants to do something in my life to bring laughter, joy, and compassion out of me that I would not have otherwise. Animals are a helper, meet and able, suitable, and sent from God to His people. You think animals will be in heaven? How could you not?

Let's look at the wisdom of the eagle:

> Doth the eagle mount up at thy command, and make her nest on high? She dwelleth and abideth on the rock, upon the crag of the rock, and the strong place (Job 39:27-28).

In other words, the nature of the eagle, her strength, and the high nest, are all attributes that God put in her. They are all aspects of the nature and the character of God that He has given to humanity—for them to see and to know Him better.

ANIMAL WISDOM 12

In Genesis, the Bible says that the serpent was more subtle than any of the beasts that God made.

"Now the serpent was more subtil than any beast of the field which the LORD God had made" (Genesis 3:1a).

Subtlety is intelligence. Cunning. Cleverness. Wisdom. The Bible says that the serpent was more subtle, more wise, more clever than the other beasts, so the other beasts were subtle and clever and smart, as well. The serpent just had more of it.

God put intelligence in animals to express His nature—just like the dogs that have a sense of smell 30,000-80,000 times greater than man's ability to smell. Animals have a God-given intelligence that has been given to serve mankind. Animals are the highest form of God's earthly creations, just below man.

"But ask now the beasts, and they shall
teach thee; and the fowls of the air, and
they shall tell thee" (Job 12:7).

Ask the beasts, and they will teach you. During the
Tsunami in Indonesia, if the people had been able to
perceive the imminent danger like the animals that
fled to higher ground, none of them would have been
killed. An expression of God to humanity was not
perceived because we were too dense to hear it. Why is
it that even when the animals give us an aspect of
God's healing, an aspect of God's wisdom, and an
aspect of God's nature, we still think that they are
"stupid animals?" God has expressed His intelligence
and His wisdom, through animals.

Animals are very intelligent. Geese fly in a "V"
formation because flying that way saves energy. We
have come to understand the aerodynamics of geese in
flight and have adapted to them, and fly that way in
military formations. It is superior aerodynamics. Who
taught them that? God. He put it in them.

A bat processes over 20,000 echo reflections per
second. That is radar. They can snatch a bug in flight.
They can locate their nesting place in total darkness.
They can elude and evade in total darkness because
they have built-in radar. They know exactly where
home is. They know exactly where to land. They know
exactly where to hit. God put it in them.

Whales and dolphins process over 200,000 echo
reflections per second with their radar. They know
where they are. They know where their prey is located,

and they know where their predators are. They know what's around them and they still function and maneuver even while swimming in dark, murky water.

I wonder how much we spend on the various radar systems in our submarine programs. Do you think ours is that good? We need to learn from animals.

Migratory birds have a built-in global positioning system (GPS). They know exactly where they are at any given time. Think about these numbers. Think about the magnitude of these achievements.

- The Grayling Goose flies 1,800 miles from Southwest Europe to Scandinavia.
- The Eurasian Crane flies 2,500 miles from Spain to the Boreal forest.
- The White Stork flies 3,100 miles from Central Africa to Western Europe.
- The Bald Eagle flies 1,800 miles from the American West to Alaska.
- The Canadian Goose flies 2,000 miles from the Gulf of Mexico to the Arctic Circle.
- The Arctic Tern flies 12,500 miles from the Arctic to the Antarctic.

That tells you about animals and what God has put in them. I believe they are special; what about you?

Now I know that there are some people who think that you should not necessarily think or talk about animals in this context, but the Bible does teach and talk a lot about it. This is one of the most intriguing things that I have ever come across.

HEAVEN: EARTH'S PATTERN 13

> Who serve unto the example and shadow of
> heavenly things, as Moses was admonished
> of God when he was about to make the
> tabernacle: for, See, saith he, that thou
> make all things according to the pattern
> shewed to thee in the mount (Hebrews
> 8:5).

We see here a man of God being instructed by the
Lord to pattern the things on the earth after the
things that are in heaven. To a degree, what you see in
heaven is what you see in the earth: the foundations of
the cities, the city foursquare, the New Jerusalem, and
its twelve precious stones. Are you ready for this?
Every one of those precious stones that are in heaven
can be found here in the earth. Gold is in the earth as
well as being in heaven's streets of gold. What you see
on the earth first came from heaven. I really don't
know how it all came to be here—or how God did all

that—but you will find on the earth the same things that you find in heaven.

Animals found on the earth are patterned after the animals found in heaven. If you find animals on the earth it is likely and probable, if not an absolute certainty, that you will find them in heaven, as well. They could be, however, in a different form. In heaven, for instance, the animals will not be in a fallen state as they are here. Animals that are in heaven now may be what animals used to look like on earth before the fall of man. What we see now in earthly animals is not an exact replica, but only a resemblance of heavenly animals because of the intrusion of sin. When you see a man in heaven in a glorified state, he will look different than a man here in a sinful state.

> It was therefore necessary that the patterns of things in the heavens should be purified with these; but the heavenly things themselves with better sacrifices than these (Hebrews 9:23).

Here it is again: what we see on the earth was patterned after what was originally, or initially, in heaven.

The question remains, "Will there be animals in heaven?" Well, I think if you didn't have any more proof than what you have right there you could answer "yes" and not be in any violation whatsoever; but we need more evidence.

BIBLICAL PROOF 14

There is a story familiar to most of you in Second Kings, chapter two, that records the Prophet Elijah's trip to heaven.

> And it came to pass, as they still went on, and talked, that, behold, there appeared a chariot of fire, and horses of fire, and parted them both asunder; and Elijah went up by a whirlwind into heaven (2 Kings 2:11).

What was his ride? It was a chariot pulled by what? Horses, that's what! He was riding in a chariot pulled by horses. From where did those horses come? They came from heaven! They were heavenly citizens. They were agents sent from heaven by God to transport one of His prophets. This proves that there are horses in heaven.

And Elisha saw it, and he cried, My father,
my father, the chariot of Israel, and the
horsemen thereof. And he saw him no
more: and he took hold of his own clothes,
and rent them in two pieces (2 Kings 2:12).

We now have horses and angels coming after the
prophet Elisha. The emphasis today, however, is not so
much on the angels, as it is emphasizing and
underscoring in our thinking, the fact that the horses
were sent from heaven. We read some illustrations
about the horses in Job 39 which show how God puts
His character and nature in His creation.

Not one form of God's creation is a full expression of
who He is, not even His greatest creation, man. Now,
we are only in part; we are not complete, in and of
ourselves. Our abilities, talents, skills, and our way of
thinking is uniquely ours; however, when we put all of
us together—all Christian people—we become the
body of Christ. Each of us brings something to the
table that gives us a full expression of who God is.

The Creator Revealed

The animal world to a degree is like that. Animals are
an expression of God's nature, even though they were
not created in His image the same way man was.

For the invisible things of him from the
creation of the world are clearly seen, being
understood by the things that are made,
even his eternal power and Godhead; so

that they are without excuse (Romans 1:20).

In other words, the expression of God is clearly seen in the things that He has created and the things that He has made—even His eternal power and Godhead—so they are without excuse. Paul is saying to the world that even if you cannot know God from the Bible, you can still know Him from His creation.

God has put instincts in the animals. We discovered earlier that geese use certain laws of physics while flying in a "V" formation, certain birds use a built-in global positioning system (GPS) to help them migrate, and the whales and other fish use their built-in sonar that God put in them, to help navigate the seas. Through the intelligence that God put in the animals, He is speaking to a lost and dying world.

The Bible teaches that if you will just look around, you will realize that no man could possibly have created the animals or given them intelligence; subsequently, you no longer have any excuse. You will not be able to stand before God in the Day of Judgment and offer the excuse that He never gave you any evidence of who He is. You cannot stand before Him and say that you did not know Him. There are no more excuses. His creation has shown His character to all of us.

As we see here, in 2 Kings, the eye of our faith sees more than our physical eye could ever possibly see, "And he answered, Fear not: for they that be with us are more than they that be with them" (2 Kings 6:16).

He was talking about the people on the earth who were facing a crisis. God was encouraging them with the fact that the number of those fighting on their side in the spirit world were of greater number than all of the soldiers in the armies that were fighting against them.

> And Elisha prayed, and said, Lord, I pray thee, open his eyes, that he may see. And the Lord opened the eyes of the young man; and he saw: and, behold, the mountain was full of horses and chariots of fire round about Elisha (2 Kings 6:17).

God divinely revealed the appearance of those heavenly horses to the people on the earth so they could physically see them. The horses were in heaven and sent to the earth for a reason.

Are there animals in heaven? Absolutely. We have determined that there are definitely horses in heaven. It just stands to reason that the other animals are there, too.

Horses in Heaven

I was talking to a guy at the gym some time ago who just didn't believe in what he characterized as "that white horse stuff." He just could not put his head around the fact that Jesus was going to come back to earth riding on a white horse. Even after I explained to him that the Bible specifically pointed that out, he thought it was nonsense. He looked at me very sincerely and said, "Well, if you really study the Bible, it's not in there." Thinking to myself, the thought came, "Well, much learning doth make thee mad!" You do not have to study very hard to figure that one out. You can simply go to one verse: Revelation 19:11.

> And I saw heaven opened, and behold a white horse; and he that sat upon him was called Faithful and True, and in righteousness he doth judge and make war (Revelation 19:11).

There is the horse! Jesus was sitting on the horse; a white horse. Jesus is the White Horse Rider.

> His eyes were as a flame of fire, and on his head were many crowns; and he had a name written, that no man knew, but he himself. And he was clothed with a vesture dipped in blood: and his name is called The Word of God. And the armies which were in heaven followed him upon white horses, clothed in fine linen, white and clean (Revelation 19:12-14).

Jesus is coming back riding on a white horse. But He is not the only one who will be coming back on a horse. Everyone who is coming back to rule and reign with Jesus will come back to Earth riding on a white horse! That means that there are an incredible number of white horses in heaven with plenty left over for the chariots. If you are not currently skilled in the art of riding horses, you will be! There are enough horses in heaven to supply a very large army. There are more than enough horses in heaven to supply all the saints of God. Everyone is going to ride a horse. It's coming!

Other Animals in Heaven?

If you look in the book of Revelation, chapter five, it deals with the saints of God in heaven after the rapture of the church.

> And one of the elders saith unto me, Weep not: behold, the Lion of the tribe of Judah, the Root of David, hath prevailed to open the book, and to loose the seven seals thereof. And I beheld, and, lo, in the midst of the throne and of the four beasts, and in the midst of the elders, stood a Lamb as it had been slain, having seven horns and seven eyes, which are the seven Spirits of God sent forth into all the earth. And he came and took the book out of the right hand of him that sat upon the throne. And when he had taken the book, the four beasts and four and twenty elders fell down before the Lamb, having every one of them harps, and golden vials full of odours, which are the prayers of saints. And they sung a new song, saying, Thou art worthy to take the book, and to open the seals thereof: for thou wast slain, and hast redeemed us to God by thy blood out of every kindred, and tongue, and people, and nation; And hast made us unto our God

kings and priests: and we shall reign on the earth (Revelation 5:5-10).

This is written in future tense. Christians have reigning in their future!

We won't wait on Jesus here on earth; we will go to heaven, experience the marriage supper of the Lamb, and then come back to reign with Him.

> And I beheld, and I heard the voice of many angels round about the throne and the beasts and the elders: and the number of them was ten thousand times ten thousand, and thousands of thousands (Revelation 5:11).

The saints in heaven are now singing a new song. You have the angels, the beasts, and the elders in heaven around the throne, with the beasts and the elders numbered 10,000 times 10,000 and thousands of thousands; the math works out to 100 million plus thousands times thousands. That is a lot. You have to remember at the time this was written, the terms "million," "billion," and "trillion" did not exist. So you have to multiply thousands times thousands. Their numbering system had not yet been developed and refined to the degree it has today and that is why you had to multiply thousands times thousands.

> Saying with a loud voice, Worthy is the Lamb that was slain to receive power, and riches, and wisdom, and strength, and

honour, and glory, and blessing. And every creature which is in heaven, and on the earth, and under the earth, and such as are in the sea, and all that are in them, heard I saying, Blessing, and honour, and glory, and power, be unto him that sitteth upon the throne, and unto the Lamb for ever and ever (Revelation 5:12-13).

We don't have a problem with saints, elders, and angels being in heaven; but, now let's add in the beasts—or animals. The word "animal" is not found in the King James Version of the Bible; you have to look in other translations to find it. Actually, a better translation of the word "beast" in the King James translation would be "living creature." So now we have the angels, the saints, the elders, and the creatures before the throne of God.

The word "living creature" or "beast" comes from the Greek word *zoon* which means "living being" or animal. It is the root word from which we get the word "zoo." We go to the zoo to see animals, don't we? This word "beast" is an Old English word that the translators put in the King James Version that would better be translated "animal."

Talking Animals

There are unquestionably animals in heaven, and they are talking! Eve heard the serpent talking, didn't she? Remember, the things on the earth are patterned after the things that are in heaven—the original became the pattern for creation. It then stands to reason, that if there are animals speaking on the earth, they are surely a reflection or an image of what exists in heaven before the sin of man took its toll.

Around the Throne

Animals in heaven are worshiping God along with the saints, angels, and the elders. They are all mixed in together. Animals were originally created by God to be companions to, companions for, helpers to, and helpers for mankind. Therefore, God sees them as a high form of creation. Animals, along with the people and the angels, were worshiping and praising God.

> And the four beasts said, Amen. And the four and twenty elders fell down and worshipped him that liveth forever and ever (Revelation 5:14).

And so here again, animals are speaking and worshiping in heaven. Quickly reading through the Scriptures will not show you that. Moreover, when we use the word "beasts" it can be a word that we hide behind. You might think that we won't know what the beasts are until we get to heaven, but that's not so— you can know now. You do not have to wait until you get to heaven, but you will have to make the effort to study in order to grasp it.

> And I beheld, and heard an angel flying through the midst of heaven, saying with a loud voice, Woe, woe, woe, to the inhabiters

of the earth by reason of the other voices of the trumpet of the three angels, which are yet to sound! (Revelation 8:13).

When one of the plagues or one of the fearful woes came to the earth, there was, according to this verse, an angel flying around heaven saying, "Woe, woe, woe." But if you look at that in another translation you will see something quite different.

The Amplified Bible says it this way:

> Then I [looked and I] saw a solitary eagle flying in midheaven, and as it flew I heard it crying with a loud voice, Woe, woe, woe to those who dwell on the earth, because of the rest of the trumpet blasts which the three angels are about to sound (Revelation 8:13, AMP).

Here is how the *Contemporary English Version* says it:

> Then I looked and saw a lone eagle flying across the sky. It was shouting, "Trouble, trouble, trouble to everyone who lives on earth! (Revelation 8:13, CEV).

The *Good News Bible* says this:

> Then I looked, and I heard an eagle that was flying high in the air say in a loud voice, "O horror! horror! How horrible it will be for all who live on earth when the

sound comes from the trumpets that the other three angels must blow! (Revelation 8:13, GNB).

Here, we can actually read in the Bible that there is a talking eagle flying around heaven! I read at least twenty translations of Revelation 8:13, and every translation I read, except for the King James Version, translates the word, not as an angel, but as an eagle. Just look up the word in any translation you desire, and it will say the same thing—eagle. This is a word that is, in fact, in the Bible. I would guess the translator of the King James did not have the courage to translate that word correctly. Eagles that talk! Eagles that worship! Imagine what heaven contains. Can you possibly imagine how much more astonishing heaven will be, if that is even possible, with the restoration of all of these beings? *The Amplified Bible* says a solitary eagle, *The Living Bible* says a solitary eagle, the NIV says an eagle. So there was an eagle flying around in heaven, talking! I don't know if all the animals in heaven can speak, but I do know that according to the Word of God, some animals in heaven can.

A NEW HEAVEN AND EARTH 15

Here is another question that always comes up, "What about extinct animals?" Most scientists agree when they tell us that at least 95-99% of all the species of animals that have ever existed on this planet are extinct today. What about them? The answer is in the book of Revelation: "And He Who is seated on the throne said, See! I make all things new" (Revelation 21:5a).

The word "new" is an important word. Sometimes the word "new" refers to something that has never existed before, like a new baby boy. Sometimes, however, it does not refer to an original, it refers to a restoration. The Scripture says, "Behold I make all things *new*." That is a different word. In this context it is a word that has to do with making something fresh or better than it was; it is a term that deals with renewal or renovation, but not creation. So when God says "I make all things new," He did not say that He was making things that never existed, He is taking what currently exists, and making it fresh, new, and pristine. He is giving it an overhaul.

In other words, there is a renovated heaven and a renovated earth that is coming. Revelation 21:1 records, "And I saw a new heaven and a new earth: for the first heaven and the first earth were passed away; and there was no more sea." This is dealing with the process of restitution. It deals with the process of redemption—to restore again to not only what it was, but to a better state than it was before the renovation. That is precisely what this word "new" means when you study it.

Another Thought

The following verses in the third chapter of Acts talk about restitution:

> Repent ye therefore, and be converted, that your sins may be blotted out, when the times of refreshing shall come from the presence of the Lord. And he shall send Jesus Christ, which before was preached unto you: Whom the heaven must receive until the times of restitution of all things, which God hath spoken by the mouth of all his holy prophets since the world began (Acts 3:19-21).

On a side note, some people believe that we have to get everything ready so that Jesus can come back. They believe that the restitution of all things will not happen until we get everything ready for Jesus to come. Some translations would lead you to believe that. I do not believe that at all; I think it is a poor translation.

When Jesus was resurrected, He was received up again into heaven. So we have not received Him where He is now. When He comes back to earth, there will be the restitution of all things. The word "restitution" is a similar word to the word meaning "made new." It deals with overhaul, redemption, and the making new from a weakened, worn-out state. The Bible says that the earth is going to wax old, just as a garment does, but Jesus will restore it and return it to its original glory, plus some.

Renovation, Restoration, and Restitution

The restitution of all things is when you have an entire, extinct species restored back to life. Dinosaurs, for instance, will return without the danger portrayed in the film, *Jurassic Park*. There will not be any concern that a Tyrannosaurus Rex will eat your car while you're in it! And you know that because of what we have read from the Old Testament in Isaiah and other places, where it talks about the lion lying down with the lamb, the leopard playing with the kid goat, the child playing over the hole of the asp or the cobra. God is going to take creation in its fallen state and restore it back to its original state.

We see eleven animals mentioned in Isaiah.

But with righteousness shall he judge the poor, and reprove with equity for the meek of the earth: and he shall smite the earth: with the rod of his mouth, and with the breath of his lips shall he slay the wicked. And righteousness shall be the girdle of his loins, and faithfulness the girdle of his reins. The wolf also shall dwell with the lamb, and the leopard shall lie down with the kid; and the calf and the young lion and the fatling together; and a little child shall lead them. And the cow and the bear shall feed; their young ones shall lie down together: and the lion shall eat straw like the ox. And the sucking child shall play on the hole of the asp, and the weaned child shall put his hand on the cockatrice' den. They shall not hurt nor destroy in all my holy mountain: for the earth shall be full of the knowledge of the Lord, as the waters cover the sea (Isaiah 11:4-9).

There is a restoration and restitution of species coming. When the devil is taken out of the picture, God's creation on the earth is restored again to where it will no longer hurt or harm anything. The animals won't kill, maim, or destroy us. I recognize that this may be new to the way we are used to thinking, but it is true, nonetheless. Just think how exciting it will be, to live on the earth with dinosaurs—without us being on an appetizer tray!

Take a look at Acts 3:21from *The Darby Bible*:

> Whom heaven indeed must receive till
> [the] times of [the] restoring of all things,
> of which God has spoken by the mouth of
> his holy prophets since time began (Acts
> 3:21, DARBY).

The *Good News Bible* says it this way:

> He must remain in heaven until the time
> comes for all things to be made new, as
> God announced through his holy prophets
> of long ago (Acts 3:21, GNB).

So, this is the process of "making new" that we saw in
Revelation. When Jesus returns, He will begin to
restore again what was fallen, what was damaged, and
what was hurt.

In the "making new" process, the animals in our
present fallen animal kingdom that hurt and devours
things, eat one another, or in some cases eat human
beings will stop their aggressive behaviors. The shark
will no longer hurt or kill you. The lion will be as
harmless as a house cat. There will be a return of the
species to not only what it was before the fall of man,
but to a better condition than ever.

AND THE ANSWER IS...   16

The big question on the mind of many people is whether or not our pets will be in heaven. Will Scooter be there? What about Maggie? Will Rogers said, "If there are no dogs in heaven, then when I die, I want to go where they went." Now that may be more sentimental and not too theological but, nonetheless, it does express how people love animals.

What Do the Theologians Say?

I want to share some quotes from some highly respected theologians who are of like-mind concerning this subject. I could give you a list of twenty of these scholars, but for the sake of simplicity, I will mention only a few. I don't want you to think that I'm on my personal soapbox talking about some isolated thought that no one else knows anything about.

> Because the creature itself also shall be
> delivered from the bondage of corruption

> into the glorious liberty of the children of God. For we know that the whole creation groaneth and travaileth in pain together until now. And not only they, but ourselves also, which have the firstfruits of the Spirit, even we ourselves groan within ourselves, waiting for the adoption, to wit, the redemption of our body (Romans 8:21–23).

Written in King James English, these passages can sometimes be a bit difficult to understand, and if you are not careful, you can read past what the Holy Spirit is saying. So let us consult these great theologians.

Noted theologian and author, Dr. William R. Newell says that we should be tender and patient toward animals which are in a dying state until our bodies and their bodies are redeemed (*Romans Verse-by-Verse*).

Dr. William L. Pettingill, Bible teacher and motivator states, "Animals generally are now suffering in the bondage of corruption. But in that day, their deliverance shall come." Do you know what that day is? That day is the coming of the Lord (*Simple Studies in Romans*).

Dr. Charles John Ellicott, a distinguished English theologian and academician of the 19th century, said this:

> The creature or creation which is the whole world of nature, animate animals and inanimate plant life wait with concentrated longing and expectancy and with groans

and travails to the future with the prospect
of joyful deliverance.

These comments are from major theologians, not just
unknown people from the back row of the church.
They are major church leaders, who throughout history
have acknowledged the fact that the animal world is
coming to a time of deliverance which will be at the
resurrection of the saints. As you can see, this is not an
isolated form of thought.

Other Notables

John Calvin, pastor and founder of Calvinism
theology, commented on verse twenty-one by saying:

> Creatures are not content in their present
> state and yet they are not so distressed that
> they pine away without the prospect of a
> remedy; a restoration to a better state that
> awaits them (*Calvin's Commentaries*, Vol.
> 38).

Let's read in Romans, the eighth chapter again:

> Because the creature itself also shall be
> delivered from the bondage of corruption
> into the glorious liberty of the children of
> God (Romans 8:21).

The creature itself shall be delivered from the bondage
of corruption and the effects of sin that have come on
this planet.

Redemption Revisited

Dr. E.D. Buckner, in his book *The Immortality of Animals* (1903) said this:

> St. Paul gives us to understand that this suffering of animals shall not be hopeless but that they shall be delivered together with man from the bondage of corruption (p. 76).

Now notice how Buckner said, "They shall be delivered together with man." Where did he get that part? Look at the latter part of verse 23, "Even we ourselves groan within ourselves, waiting for the adoption, to wit, the redemption of our body" (Romans 8:23b). Let's examine this truth in detail.

When does the redemption of our body happen? First Thessalonians, chapter four says that it is at the resurrection of the saints. This is talking about the redemption and the resurrection of the body.

> For the Lord himself shall descend from heaven with a shout, with the voice of the archangel, and with the trump of God: and the dead in Christ shall rise first: Then we who are alive and remain shall be caught up together with them in the clouds to meet the Lord in the air. And thus we shall always be with the Lord (1 Thessalonians 4:16-17).

Notice the word "creature" back in the book of Romans, chapter eight:

> Because the creature itself also shall be delivered from the bondage of corruption into the glorious liberty of the children of God (Romans 8:21).

This verse indicates a resurrection of the animals. Resurrection of the animals happens at the same time the saints are resurrected. I didn't write that verse; it was authored by the Apostle Paul writing by the inspiration of the Holy Spirit.

Why is it written in that context if it does not mean the resurrection of the animals? The corruption and the bondage of the animal world remains until the saints are resurrected. At the resurrection of the saints, the animal world is freed. "But that doesn't necessarily mean that Fido is going to heaven," you say. Let's look more closely at the resurrection mentioned here.

It seems that the animals are delivered when we get our new bodies at the resurrection. It appears to happen at the same time.

> All flesh is not the same flesh: but there is one kind of flesh of men, another flesh of beasts, another of fishes, and another of birds (1 Corinthians 15:39).

The word used here to describe the flesh is the Greek word *sarx*, which is the same exact word found in the third chapter of Luke, "And all *flesh* shall see the salvation of God" (Luke 3:6).

All flesh, all *sarx*, which we just said were fish, birds, beasts, and men. Remember the word "beasts" means living creatures or animals. All flesh shall see the salvation of God. This is a first-rate proof text. I am building a case to take away any doubts.

Isaiah writes, "The glory of Lord shall be revealed and all *flesh* shall see it together for the mouth of the Lord hath spoken it" (Isaiah 40:5). That is a pretty potent Bible verse, isn't it? All flesh. Do you know how much flesh is left out of the word "all"? None. So, does the Bible speak of the deliverance of the animals? It absolutely does. And when does it say that it will happen? The resurrection of the saints indicates a resurrection of the animals, too.

Clinching the Nail

With the plethora of information that we have looked at thus far, we have "driven the nail pretty deep in the board," having a confidence that there are, in fact, animals in heaven. Now we're going to bring permanence to this knowledge and clinch that nail on the backside. When you clinch a nail, you drive the nail through the wood until the head is buried and the sharp end is sticking out on the backside. You then take your hammer and bend the sharp end over until it is somewhat buried in the backside of the board. That is the process of clinching the nail. That nail is not coming out, and as a result, our wondering will no longer be an issue.

These are significant passages of scripture in Psalms that give us additional glimpses into God's character.

> O Lord, how manifold are thy works! in wisdom hast thou made them all: the earth is full of thy riches. So is this great and wide sea, wherein are things creeping innumerable, both small and great beasts. There go the ships: there is that leviathan, whom thou hast made to play therein. These wait all upon thee; that thou mayest give them their meat in due season (Psalms 104:24–27).

Many translators translate *leviathan* as "sea monster" which is, in actuality, a large ocean animal that is possibly like a great whale or a giant squid. No one knows for sure. It is simply a large sea creature that plays in the ocean. These animals roam the ocean, and you are the one that feeds and provides for them.

> That thou givest them they gather: thou openest thine hand, they are filled with good. Thou hidest thy face, they are troubled: thou takest away their breath, they die, and return to their dust (Psalms 104:28-29).

This is a picture of the animals after the fall of man. This was not what God really wanted; death is a result of sin. These creatures go to the sea and God feeds them, but just like man, they have their finite time on the earth and then they die.

We go on to read in Psalms, "Thou sendest forth thy spirit, they are created: and thou renewest the face of the earth" (Psalms 104:30).

Do you understand what that just said? When God visits this planet again by His Spirit, the dead animals are created, renewed, and brought back to life. This is talking about resurrection. God has clearly said in His Word that not only will there be animals in heaven, but the indication is that the dead animals will be restored to life, as well.

> And he will love thee, and bless thee, and multiply thee: he will also bless the fruit of thy womb, and the fruit of thy land, thy corn, and thy wine, and thine oil, the increase of thy kine, and the flocks of thy sheep, in the land which he sware unto thy fathers to give thee. Thou shalt be blessed above all people: there shall not be male or female barren among you, or among your cattle (Deuteronomy 7:13-14).

Notice that He said that this covenant blessing would rest on the child of God. I heard one theologian say that he believed that only the animals of the saints would be revived because of His covenant with them;

he didn't believe all of them would be. The Bible, however, seems to indicate a different position—that all species of all animals will be resurrected.

Yes, Our Pets Will Be in Heaven

I am confident that the animals of Christians are going to be in heaven. Will my dog be in heaven? I believe he will be. Will your cat be there? I am sure she will—the dogs will have to have something to chase!

John Wesley said:

> Something better remains after death for the poor creatures. That these likewise shall one day be delivered from this bondage of corruption and shall then receive an ample amends for all their present sufferings.

Joni Erickson Tada, artist and Christian speaker, had this to say:

> If God brings our pets back to life, it wouldn't surprise me. It would be just like Him. It would be totally in keeping with His generous character, exorbitant, excessive, extravagance in grace after grace. Oh, for all the dazzling discoveries and ecstatic pleasures Heaven will hold for us, the potential of seeing 'Scrappy' would be your whimsy; utterly joyful, surprisingly superfluous. Heaven is going to be a place

that will refract and reflect in as many ways as is possible, the goodness and joy of our great God, who delights in lavishing love on His children.

When Billy Graham was asked if there would be animals in heaven, or if our pets would go, he said that God wanted His people happy and if having their animals in heaven would make them happy, he supposed that there was a reason to believe that they would be there.

We now have a convincing theological and biblical record that there absolutely will be animals in heaven. I believe the combination of the biblical evidence and the irrefutable historical record of these well-respected theologians unquestionably proves to us that there will be animals in heaven, and it makes our case airtight.

I believe that your pets will be there, as well.

ABOUT THE AUTHOR

 **DR. ED KING** is the founder and Senior Pastor of Redemption Church in Knoxville, Tennessee. In addition to pastoring, Dr. King is president of *The Power of the Word* television ministry, which is broadcast both nationally and internationally to a potential audience of over one billion people. He resides in Knoxville along with his wife and co-pastor, Nora. Their daughter Laren and son-in-law Adam also work with them in full-time ministry. In addition to pastoring Redemption Church and his lead role at *Power of the Word*, Pastor King travels extensively, and he has ministered in over sixty nations around the world, teaching, and preaching the gospel to thousands of people in leadership conferences and evangelistic meetings.

redemptionchurch

For additional products or scheduling information, please contact:

3550 Pleasant Ridge Road ✤ Knoxville, TN 37921 USA

Tel: 865.521.7777 or 800.956.4433

www.RedemptionChurch.com

CONTACT US

RedemptionChurchTN   RedemptionChurchTN   @RedemptionTN

MORE BOOKS BY DR. ED KING

How to Be Twice As Happy

Are you happy? When everything goes according to plan...when everything works exactly like we want it to...when life is good, it's easy to be happy. Life, however, can and does throw many things our way that cause our happiness quotient to decrease dramatically. In this book Dr. King shares twenty important keys to true happiness.

Cause & Effect: Staying Free From the Curse

Jesus redeemed us from the curse of the law. Dr. King teaches you how to stay free from the curse of the law and live in God's blessings.

10 Major Life Lessons—CD series

This series will upgrade your life in every way. You'll learn the power of a seed, the importance of forgiveness, how to live a disciplined life, and much more. Apply these valuable ten lessons to your own life, and you'll go further than you ever thought possible.

Conquering Life's Limitations—CD series

As Christians, we have the mind of Christ and there are no limitations on what God can reveal and show to you if we're open to it. Listen as Pastor Nora King explains how wisdom is the most important thing to us if we want to conquer life's limitations.

Divine Healing and the Atonement—CD series

Do you need healing in your life? Are you aware of the healing power that is available to you? In Pastor King's message, you can discover: the true meaning of Jesus' atonement, and how Jesus satisfied the judgement against us to bring us righteousness and healing

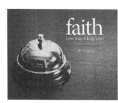

Faith: How May It Help You?—CD series

God never intended for His family to live a life of lack, struggle or constant defeat. He sent His Word to rescue us and He gave FAITH as a tool to overcome the obstacles we face. We can take the gift of faith, and by activating it and using it, we can create an exciting and victorious life.

Grace vs. Works—CD series

For by grace we are saved through faith—it is a gift of God, not of works. Grace verses works—they both have to be looked at; they have to be thought about; and they have to be considered. Both are biblical truths and are important to believers.

Heaven—CD series
We hear a lot about Heaven. What does the Bible say about it? This 11-part series establishes a foundational truth on our future home. Heaven is a real place; a place to look forward to. Insightful teachings like these are a must for every believer.

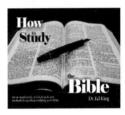
How to Study the Bible—CD series
Every Christian knows it's good to read the Bible; but, how often do we understand the depths of what we're reading? In this series, you'll learn some of the personal study habits and recommended study tools of a man with 30 years of experience in learning the Bible and a ministry for teaching.

Keeping Hope Alive—CD series
In this series, the importance of keeping hope alive is revealed, along with many ways we misplace our hope and how to break through the bondage of despair. You will also discover that hope is a vital part of who you are in Christ.

Truth: Your Baseline for Life—CD series
Listen to this 5-CD series by Pastor Ed King and discover how truth relates to your freedom, relationships, growth in character, wisdom, and much more. You can begin today to live a life of power and liberty.

Walking in Divine Favor—CD series
In this CD series, Pastor Ed King teaches keys to living in favor with God and man. Learn the importance of honor and integrity in relationships, cheerful giving, grateful receiving, and more. The keys listed in this insightful series will move you forward faster than you can move yourself alone.

Parsons Publishing House
Your Voice Your World™

WILL MY PET BE IN HEAVEN? by Dr. Ed King
We adore our pets, and they become family; so, when they pass on, we suffer great loss. Dr. Ed King gives us solid, biblical answers to this often asked question. He shows us from the Bible about the past, current, and future existence of animals in heaven, as well as their ultimate purpose. Finally, an exhaustive answer for a question that always comes up!
ISBN: 9781602730687 • 93 pages • $8.95.

30 DAYS TO A BETTER PRAYER LIFE
by Pastor Nora King
Nora King offers fresh revelation and practical teaching to help you experience the release of God's power. You will learn daily how to improve your prayer life and enter God's presence through these simple principles. You don't have to struggle in prayer any longer! ISBN: 9781602730120 • 142 pages • $11.95.

STL | Distribution
North America

CAPTURING THE HEART OF GOD
by Diane Parsons

God created man for His good pleasure. Our most satisfying goal should be to bring delight to our heavenly Father. Make it your goal today to do those things which please God. This book contains practical tips on capturing God's heart and becoming His delight everyday.
ISBN: 9781602730182 • 140 pages • $10.95 USD.

SURVIVING THE CHALLENGES OF TRANSITION
by Dr. Gerald Doggett

Dr. Gerald Doggett exhorts the reader in his second book to not let their past dictate their future. He provides exciting nuggets which include: It's OK to Remain A Chair!, Your Dream Will Attract Favor & Warfare, God Restores Everything That Has Been Lost!, and Sometimes You Need to Have A Party!
ISBN: 9781602730182 • 140 pages • $12.95 USD.

NEXT LEVEL: RAISING THE STANDARD OF GRACE
by Pastor Robert Gay

In this book, Robert is sounding a trumpet call from heaven, engaging the reader to see the Ten Commandments afresh from the empowering view of God's Grace. Robert clearly and biblically explains how Grace empowers us to live godly, holy lives above sin. There is no limit to the success, prosperity, and blessings that will surround you when you apply these principles.
ISBN: 9781602730427 • 216 pages • $14.95 USD.

INFUSE—ACTIVATING HEAVEN ON EARTH
by Dr. Kevin Bordeaux

This book will guide you in your understanding of how to have a living, dynamic relationship with God and then spread that relationship to the world. Jesus told us to pray, "On earth as it is in heaven." To do this, we must know what is happening in heaven. The Book of Revelation is not only a futuristic, apocalyptic account, but a glimpse into heaven. It is also a glimpse into how our lives can be funnels where the world can experience heaven daily through us. ISBN: 9781602730113 • 138 pages • $12.95 USD.

EMERGING AS AN INNOVATIVE LEADER
by Dr. Darrell Parsons

Ideas become the catalyst for change, and change becomes the catalyst for innovation. Innovation is centered on creating or enhancing value. With this understanding, Dr. Parsons is able to concisely articulate twelve competencies which are imperative for today's innovative leader. When dealing with any group emerging leaders can begin the process leadership development by working on the competencies identified in this book.
ISBN: 9781602730649 • 228 pages (HB) • $24.95 USD.

WHY DO I DO THE THINGS I DO?
Understanding Personalities by Dr. Darrell Parsons

In this insightful book, Darrell Parsons identifies the four primary types of personalities and how they interact together. As you grow in understanding, you will gain the tools you need for developing successful relationships in all areas of your life.
ISBN: 9781602730199 • 132 pages • $10.95 USD.

RELEASE YOUR WORDS—IMPACT YOUR WORLD
by Dr. Darrell Parsons

Your words can make a difference! God has placed treasures inside you; learn to release them to influence your world. In this book, Darrell Parsons challenges you to use your voice to impact the world around you today.
ISBN: 9781602730007 • 140 pages • $9.95 USD.

SONSHIP: THE MANTLE. THE JOURNEY. THE DOUBLE-PORTION
by Pastor Joshua Gay

In this book, Robert is sounding a trumpet call from heaven, engaging the reader to see the Ten Commandments afresh from the empowering view of God's grace. Robert clearly and biblically explains how grace empowers us to live godly, holy lives above sin. There is no limit to the success, prosperity, and blessings that will surround you when you apply these principles.
ISBN: 9781602730526 • 180 pages • $12.95 USD.